INTERMINABLE
PERILOUS
WATERFALLS

LILLIE JOHNSON

authorHOUSE®

AuthorHouse™
1663 Liberty Drive
Bloomington, IN 47403
www.authorhouse.com
Phone: 833-262-8899

Published by AuthorHouse 03/05/2021

ISBN: 978-1-6655-1922-9 (sc)
ISBN: 978-1-6655-1925-0 (e)

Print information available on the last page.

This book is printed on acid-free paper.

Scripture quotations marked KJV are from the Holy Bible, King James Version (Authorized Version). First published in 1611. Quoted from the KJV Classic Reference Bible, Copyright © 1983 by The Zondervan Corporation.

CONTENTS

ACKNOWLEDGEMENTS

May God bless every person who reads one of my books.
I hope it brings a little comfort to you during these weakened times.
I pray God gives us strength to come together in love
for mankind. May His spirit be the inner force.
For us to not put away hate but destroy it from the roots of hell

A MOTHER'S CHILD

You try your best with their upbringing.

Alone or with dad, into tiny ears be kind and the best at whatever you do.

Sometimes these little one is not listening, stops them from going through.

Prayers are all a mother has for them.

Son or daughter, my cries YHWH has heard and He stands with stretched out arms.

If I were going to write a book, it would be filled with heartbreaking poems.

Wanting better for them before tiny cells are being formed.

Hoping the wrong paths their feet detour.

So many tears, if only they could wash away troubles that awaits them at life's door.

Few times being disrespected, a mothers' aching heart into pieces falls to the floor.

Continual prayers to the FATHER, with thankfulness that no matter, my child is secure.

Caught in this crooked system, it is judges, appointed lawyers are full of cows manure.

Hard life growing in the hood, black skin, points taken, justice was not between the lines

Of his sentenced brochure.

What's change from yesterday? Equality for me remains obscure.

Coming into this world needing, birth certificate, ss#, your identity still darkened skin,

Labeled no worth!

Lies from the pits of hell, do not believe.

My child, upon your arrival the angels sang praises for a blessed jewel being unearth!

A mother carries her child for nine months, all her travails, she forgets at birth.

It does not matter if it is her second, third or first.

Stones pile against you already.

Trust in God always with or without your mom or daddy.

Life windowpanes says you are beaten.

Do not listen to its lies or the worlds overbearing injustices that tries to weaken.

Do not get discouraged, your black skin is not a curse, but an amazing beacon.

No matter how many thrown rocks and waterfalls of hate, the inner you is a well-of love

That makes your bitter life a little sweetened.

Knowing in all situations God is our only hopeful reasons.

I want the very best for you in all the good you do.

In life my child, there are many injustices your feet must walk through.

Stay on the right path God got you.

With whatever tools life hits, you with remember to bend your knees and ask God to anoint your soul.

Through every storm and life threating waterfalls, God is always in control.

One set or two sets of footprints in His precious bosom your heart He holds.

Every scratched knee, broken heart, injustices, tried by and through the fire, the outcome refined gold.

We will spend eternity with the great I Am.

For now, …

I cannot blanket you from hurt and pain, but I can cover you with blood of the Lamb.

Hold on look beyond those barricades and bricks stacked in a pile.

Listen to His peaceful voice that says we will be together in a little while.

This truth should give you hope daily and make your heart smile.

My prayers to God if I am no longer here, take care of my child.

A MOTHER'S OASIS

Love is the foundation she placed underneath their feet.
The chambers of their heart's continual prayers of laughter and honesty.
Book of truth accepting old sayings "death you can't cheat".
Before the break of dawn, shoes on mind tired and body weak.
Being both parents, no time- outs looking in their eyes is my motivation
I am strong even though aching and beat.
Thanks to the Father always for falling crumbs her children had food
to eat.
Cleaning other people' homes, miles on your body, blistered hands and
feet.
Silent prayers to Him for enough rest within the few hours she would sleep.
Strength and endurance Father this job I need to keep.
Speedily walking like a snail in the rain
Headed home to the many holes in a falling shack.
Spare boards and canvas another leak she tars and tacks.
Kneeling at her baby's bed kissing their foreheads and rubbing their backs.
Sitting down in an old chair that is lost its cushion, mostly wood.
Blessings along her roughed path, tending to her babies like a loving
mother should.
Tears of praises to the Father for the bad and good.
I taught them the word of YAH with little and doing my best.
Seeds I planted into their souls, I hope they keep no longer being in the
nest.
Prayers to the Father daily before breakfast and getting dressed.
Through everything we have always been blessed.

Sitting in my old chair smiling tiny hands and feet, giving thanks during storms more or less.

A life of struggles never alone and Father, up this roughed mountain I do not regret.

Our nothing in the eyes of others, was blooming bowls of oats and grains.

Into our lives within the wind's contentment remained.

Upon our mountains of disaster Your mercy came.

Father not one time have I been ungrateful or complained.

Love is what You poured in Your drops of rain.

Little was nothing to hide or be ashamed.

Father, You always answered when I called Your name.

Heartfelt moments and letting go of life' hand, if possible, Lord there's nothing I'd changed.

Being a single mother was not pointing fingers at their dad or blame.

Prayers and thankfulness were the fuel to our burning flame.

Helping others no matter what the situation I targeted I aimed.

Hard work and holding His hand have been the plan.

Today tears of loss I do understand.

I am crying through all of this; my faith keeps me from letting go of His hand.

Questions I erase from my hurting heart, knowing He'll give me strength to stand.

Thanking Him for much when it was so little.

Through their colds, flu, broken hearts, not once admitted in the hospital.

Worked till my skin is wrinkled, limbs weak and brittle.

Will the sunshine for me over here or looking at family photos over there?

I am running and looking finding no comfort anywhere.

Father my tears are overwhelming waterfalls, do You care?

My little ones are gone, I am sitting on and old cushion- less chair.

I am sad eyes open heart beating Your instruction and cannot find the route.

What is this all about?

I am alone goes deeper than combined seasons of drought.

Father I am not complaining because You always helped me out.

Tiny hands and feet like history, their smiles and dreams fading traces.

They are gone Father I will never hold their hands or kiss their faces.

This old house and their memories have filled all the open spaces.
Thank You Father do not know if I am sincere.
Forgive me for my anger because they are not here.
You have them, those seeds I planted have reached heavens' door.
All their laughter I hope You let the clouds pour.
Into my heart I know the little You gave was always more.
My heart is aching, mind full and eyes sore.
They are finally free.
Falling ashes poured under their favorite oak tree.
There is no path that will lead them back to me.
The seeds planted, His presence and love they now see.
My prayers into the chess of eternity they have the key.
Father, thank You this is how I wanted it to be.
My tears will turn to joy and laughter.
This life I will soon be with You in the hereafter.
My present tears of sadness are temporarily.
Playful laughter being pushed on a swing, seeing how high they go.
Sun is bright, Spring is here birds singing goodbye to Winters' snow.
Sitting in my cushion-less chair looking out my cracked windowpane, seeds planted its roots
of children' love did grow.
In the front yard flowers not blooming, stems and crying petals hang low.
Balls in the shade needing a child' hand to throw.
My heart crying because of dying meadows.
Father, what I do know...
Heaven got four angels a week ago.
Wishful thinking a little time with them You'd let me borrow.
Truth be told it is my season of sorrow.
Looking, they are gone into the heavens like a fading shadow.
I am sitting here waiting for a gentle laugh or peaceful hello.
That old oak tree with a swing on it has been replaced by a weeping willow.
I am alone, all that I planned for them I am the one left holding a teary soaked pillow.

BABIES WHO DID NOT ASK TO BE BORN

———————————❦———————————

Babies who did not ask to be born
You say I was a mistake you could not care for me.
Yet you laid down and had three.
You ripped me from God's hand.
I was thrown away because you did not have a plan.
I never had a chance to run sit or stand.
You said having me would make you lose your shape.
You put me in a box and sealed me with tape.
Oh, mother dear you did not want me because you were raped.
I was dismissed because I was too much on your plate.
Me oh my I was conceived on your third date.
You got rid of me. I never got to live in the city or state.
I was too heavy you could not carry the load.
So, you flushed me down the commode.
I wonder if the decision you made will your soul be haunted.
I was thrown away because you said I was not wanted.
Not (even) giving me to another.
You were in control supposing to be a loving mother.
We were twins not a chance a sister or brother.
I would have been a bouncing baby boy.
My dreams you took away and my life you destroyed.
Not giving me a chance to experience joy!
I would have made a difference in the world,

She will never know I was a girl.
I was conceived while my mother slept
I was murdered because my name was burden no one kept.
I had no funeral not one soul wept!
I was not worth more than the trash on the floor she swept
no one sounded a trumpet or horn.
Every day we are being destroyed ripped and torn!
Babies who did not ask to be born!

BLACK FLOWER

High school sweethearts' different sides of the track.
His parents had everything; my parents were content.
Mitchell pushing me on a tire swing, grandpa made for me.
We were happier in my back yard, than his miles of pool.
His mother's beautiful peaceful garden, so amazingly breath-taking.
His house, my house and yard could fit, and still have room.
I met his parents once and that was enough, for their son they
Wanted more and the things needed for me, to have their son,
Would have drained my soul.
I was respectful and kind because they were not, especially his mother.
She treated me like I had a disease.
In her eyes I would not measure up.
In Mitchell's heart I made him full.
I thank God for him.
I can hear grandpa saying it will be just fine, my black flower.
I would not want to be ears in the corner of their house, when my
Name was mentioned.
We love each other and vowed to wait for each other.
The true stories my grandparents' told Mitchell, he loved
Me more for being a part of my family.
Bouquet of flowers weekly sat on my mother's table.
With his new schedule for school, chores and work, bouquet,
Was replaced, with three different color roses in a small vase.
Thank you note for my grandparents, for their shared experiences.
Time never stops, he is away at college his senior year.

I am a cashier at the only retail supermarket store.
Mother misses the weekly roses, her table is naked, so I pick her daisies.
It's lonesome here without him making grandpa laugh. I am taking care of my
Grandparents and helping with the bills we are ok, emails
Mailbox letters, a book about our lives blooming.
Face chat grandpa, he asked when are you going to marry black flower?
Mitchell said soon.
His plane landed at 4:00 o'clock, grandma is in the hospital
From the airport to room 4444, and a bouquet of white roses. Grandma said…
Mitchell take care of our angel; she loves you so much.
He hugged and kissed her on the cheek, a trail of tears behind her smile
She held Mitchell's face in her weak wrinkled hands, whispering I love you
This is not goodbye she smiled, looked at me and closed her eyes.
That weekend, he called his parents and said he would be sleeping
On the couch at my parents' house.
But he slept in grandpa's room on the chair.
We buried grandma that Monday.
She was 109 years Young, they married when she was 14 years old.
I did not see her ring on her finger, grandpa said it is OK.
Another weekend, and Mitchell's sleeping on the chair.
Mom made dinner, a bouquet of never seen green roses,
On the table.
After saying grace, Mitchell asked my parents if he could have my hand
In marriage, grandpa, said yes, Lord yes.
Mom and dad laughed.
You can marry black flower.
He placed the ring on my finger, it looked familiar, no
I cannot grandpa, that was grandma's ring, resize for me.
Take this token of our love and keep it in your heart.
Prayerfully you two will share more than 95 years together.
That was the longest week of my life, I did not complain because,
Mitchell lay at the foot of grandpa's bed, did not go home.
I called his mother; it was the hardest call to make.
With all the money, pools and finest clothes, her son enjoyed

That wooden shack and pond that was shared by our neighbors.
Grandpa gave him a pair of old jeans and fishing pole, sandwiches
And his tackle box, I do not know if he was reliving something he wanted,
Or spending time with grandpa because he was grieving. Whichever I
Know he loved grandpa. The sun going down and that old wrinkled
Hat and fishing pole coming up the road, they make it to the yard would
Stand there looking at the stars and later go in the shed, having no fish.
I guess
That was not the point. My loving fiancé was transforming into an angel with
No wings when grandpa talked with him, he was like a sponge, it made grandpa
Happy, the next morning he went to his house. Told his parents we are getting
Married, Mitchell had a surprise for me, I was not allowed to see till it was time.
We rehearsed the wedding, both our parents were there in our back yard, preacher
Grandpa happier than I have seen him, through many tears after grandma's passing.
His mom the maid of honor, and grandpa the best man.
He said our vows with each rose given to me and their meanings.
Multicolor roses when I saw you at school that is what you brought to
My gloomy life, colors of love, joy, mystery, excitements, friendship.
Ivory rose, the first day I saw you helping that old lady at the supermarket
And you were off from work. I was hypnotized by your petals of care
And thoughtfulness for someone who did not ask for your help.
Yellow rose, I was a little jealous, I wanted to be in the presence of
The love and warmth you put on that elderly ladies' face; I wanted your
Hand in friendship.
Lavender rose, because at that moment I fell in love with this angel.
White rose is for you keeping yourself for me only.
Peach rose, is for being born within a family of genuinely loving roots.
Orange rose, I am so proud that you chose me to share our lives.
Pink rose, I look at the chandelier with its diamonds and gold that mother
had special made for

Our dining room, and silkiest curtains made with the prettiest materials
And you are more precious and elegant that a mansion filled with these.
Green rose are seeds for our family, hopefully a little girl just like you.
Blue rose, our days will be waterfalls of joy and laughter and when
The dark clouds hover, our petals of prayer, faith and love will help
Us withstand.
Red rose, I promise to love us always, and keep myself for you only.
Black rose, I was not living with all my wealth until my heart started
To beat when it entered your presence, being here I was surrounded by pure
Treasures, that money cannot buy, your priceless smile, your tears of love
for others,
Your heart that gives when others sometimes make you cry, your persistence
To shed light, when surrounded by darkness., your perseverance.
I love you with every petal seeing an unseen of me.
I stand before God and take you for my wife to make this incomplete boy
A man-husband and from this day forth plant a garden of hope and
love, for
Our children and hand it to them so the cycle will not break.
He kissed the bride.
He gave grandpa a black rose and thanked him for all his life experiences,
Being a black man and surviving to tell another Young hungry soul with
A planting heart to do all and then more.
Later, I overheard grandpa talking to my in-laws, this is it, I hope
You accept my granddaughter; she truly is a beautiful black flower and
loving rose.
He put his arms around them and said it do not matter what side of the
Tracks you are from because its trials from the beginning leads us here
Having or not having gone through what I did and our other
Brothers and sisters who were all sacrificed, from the outhouse to many
houses
We have now, neither of us are more, we are all the same.
It is what is in our foolish imagination that separates us, but the shed blood
connects us always,
It is our trail's history, heritage, you can deny, do not accept it but the
truth is we
Are all black.

It took years before his parents accepted us, even after their beautiful
Grandchildren were born. Wisdom is precious, Mitchell and I thank God for
Grandpa who was filled with love and wisdom.
He died at 11:59 pm, (our wedding day), at the Young Age of 111.
He got to enjoy the day he prayed for all those years, for his black flower.
He and grandma were together for 95 years, a lesson that married and all
Others can learn with God, unconditional love, faith you can endure, they did not die because
Of old age, they both were in their right mind, getting around slower, but they
Knew who sustained their lives, and it was time for them to let go, leaving him
Here a month longer because there were seeds that needed to be planted.
My parents followed him two years later, they were not here as long.
Today his parents will get to spend time with the children again.
Like grandpa said it takes time for certain seeds to sprout, with love and Patience
All things in its due seasons. We are still watching seeds grow he planted.
On grandma's tombstone are red roses.
We place a bouquet of black roses on his tombstone, for the life he passed on.
Grandpa's room, he did not make any changes, sometimes he sleeps in grandpa's chair.
That old shack has been replaced with newer plywood floors and walls, ceiling
Blue paint, new windows, more rooms, we have had to replace that tire a couple of times,
Added another one in the front yard to grandpa's favorite oak.
Five more in the back yard for each Child,
The garden is filled with life blooming black roses.
The Kids enjoy going to the pond, and all the repeated stories, great- grandpa Told Mitchell.
Mitchell planted saluting multicolor roses on both sides of our walkway.
That old wooden shack, brings back beautiful memories, growing up
And new ones each day, we would not trade for a house filled with gold.

My in-laws are amazed at our shack, (home) its beautiful garden and how peaceful it is.
We sit on the porch in the swing that Mitchell built, on our all-around porch.
His mother said, I have never seen anything more beautiful.
Drinking homemade lemonade and eating bologna sandwhiches and watching my,
Grandkids play, and the petals of waving flowers and their sweet-smelling fragrances.
Grandparents would hold my hand, with every wrinkle there was a lifetime of stories.
I would hold his hand next to my face and cry.
He would say I prayed and asked God not let our past be your future.
I love them more than my parents, my parents are beautiful, but I wanted
To be in the presence of their love, the maturity of their faith in God amazed
Me as a Child and Young Lady. Every moment with them was precious.
Hate was the air that greeted them being black, but God's love is what they inhaled
And endured, I truly believe that is why they were given life at their ages.
I miss them more than my parents. I close my eyes and feel their touch.
Grandpa prayers are answered when I look at Mitchell our 5 children.
That bond that God has joined us together, I am so happy and blessed
To have someone who loves me beyond the waterfalls of life.
I look at that tire in the front yard, the wind giving it a push, and a
Little girl named Chloe, laughing, and asking grandpa to push me higher.
Grandpa saying, I love you always my beautiful black flower.
My prayers are for your life to be filled with flowers.
Because your petals deserve all the love, the heavens have for you on earth.
Your roots are compassion, empathy, that extra mile of kindness, and a heart
That goes beyond the waterfalls of life for others.
Your heart, black flower, is what keeps mines beating.
I love you grandpa.
Your black flower, misses you.

BLACK PROOF

History repeats itself, black faces of injustices the mirror of life reflects the truth.

Hopelessness and its petals are watered-down tears that continue to grow.

If the white race is superior to all, why not delete the black keys on a broken piano?

There is no need for soulful music, blue skies, or a beautiful rainbow.

Xmas should be year-round, a world filled with the whitest snow.

Colorful flowers should not bloom, just plain white petals in a row.

If God is white, why create other races, mistreated, unloved in a world, where seeds of

Hateful racism is at every open door?

Why allow us to be slaves,

Leaving us with no peaceful home to go?

Why overboard disease, broken blacks they throw?

Cemetery of black bodies are seen through opened windows.

Why give different shades of skin.

If we are slaughtered, like a herd of pigs in a pen.

Committing the same crime, or no crime at all, the white man is the one You defend.

When awaken, why are our lives a heartbreaking sequel?

If You love us,

Why aren't all races equal?

Our race injustice does as it often pleases.

Taking black lives like coughs and contagious sneezes.

Racism is thicker than Artic snow when it freezes.

I have love for all caring people.
It is hard, so very hard to accept,
In truths mirror to be forsaken by the Lord.
We obeyed Your word,
We did not spare the rod or spoil the Child.
Truth be told, beaten with injustice rod, took away their smile.
If counted for the deaths of injustice blacks, it would lead a doorway
To heaven stacked in a pile.
Our life as a vapor, poof.
If we must shout it from the highest roof.
Black lives matter.
Birthed through a black womb,
We pressed on.
Blistered hands, broken backs, picking miles of your money-making
cotton.
Traveling the path of a race that is victimized and downtrodden.
Innocent blood cries penetrated in the heart of the earth,
Restless soul's will not be forgotten.
Future to come, injustices and its many faces will be burned, buried and
rotten.
Through Jim Crow laws and all others, we are still here 2020.
From the back of the bus, to black faces driving us.
Tilling the land for others, today some of us own.
Broken chains from around our ankles, necks, and wrist.
Whips and chains generations of abuse, we will never forget.
Colored, Negros, African Americans, Blacks, we are labeled.
Better housing for their animals living in stables.
Blood and sweat, worked like a mule, given falling crumbs from their table.
Through it all we are able.
Against window's panes of beautiful waterfalls, hopeful black noses.
Tear gas, torches, dogs, burning crosses, and blasting hoses.
Our faith, field of dreams and colorful roses.
Perseverance, no matter how many time justice' door closes.
History repeats itself, black faces of injustices the mirror of life reflects
the truth,
Dying roots of racism, hatred injustice laws and fallen facades.

Through God's eyes we are the salt of the earth.
Multiple times you tried to brainwash of our worth.
Each death committed because of our blackness,
The angels planted seeds of our rebirth.
Every unjust trial, every whelp, all those hateful things we did not deserve.
In God's foreseen garden, laughter, tears of joy and rainbows of love,
And peace He preserved.
Please know, God said…
In our seasons of hopelessness, our tears, and endless miles of pain
He did not forsake but observed.
Today the wind sings "I'm sorry"
Black lives matter!
We are not going anywhere.
From the garage, to the ghetto, cardboard box, top of the hill, valley, and highest roof!
Black Proof

BLACK ROCK

I see hurt has its inward claws within, running trying to find light
When darkness' shadow blinds your sight.
Loving him more you've lost the will to fight.
Getting into this ring daily, no means of escape.
Eyes closed, hands cuffed, mouth taped.
Your rainbow has linings of gray.
You're on a merry-go-round of pain, at the end of each heartbreaking day.
There's no need for a doctor or priest.
Your mind is made up…hearts' chambers entwined to this unloving
selfish beast.
Tears from its ocean of hurt, chained in darkness, no light of being released.
The doors are shut, happiness and clouds of joy have ceased.
Foolishly dreaming he'll someday hold only me.
Momentarily steams of peace.
Your days of holding hands walking along the beach is as close as the
North to the East.
You make yourself believe a lie; my prayers God will answer.
I signed the contract of my soul, being his lifetime private dancer.
Ocean black, waves thick, and deadly.
Angels rejoicing. your diagnosis…removable cancer.
Leave it be, he's the man I love.
Eyes open, mind clear, body beaten with a sand filled sock.
Windows open doors unlocked.
The love I have for him is anchored to the bottom of maybe's dock.
A chance for him to someday truly love me, and release the hitting sands'

Within the stitches of this hurtful sock.
My bruises are deeper than the waters, with arms fragile and weak.
It's hits I try to block.
I don't know…holding on, maybe something tragic happened to me as a child,
I'm in shock?
I do love him, 2 bullets…1 soul…one gun.
Calmly cocked.
Before the sun rises into infinity, from this life we'll be blocked.
I don't know what you see, nor am I starring at the minute hand on my life' clock.
I'm ok, he's mines…not your
Black Rock

BLACK SKIN

Tears fall for a dying race in this world.
Lives taken, so many unanswered every boy and girl.
Given opportunities for living, odds better if God made us hogs.
Their world our life less than dogs.
Prayers seems beaten by their unjust laws.
Everything is out in the open, land of plenty we are dying straws.
Justice we plead, their answer "shut-up"
Whites in the front, blacks not allowed to drink from equality's cup.
Preachers saying have faith.
Our younger generation "it's too late".
For our lives," White Supremacists" dictate.
Nothing changed, 2020 and we are still handed the same hateful plate.
Being told we are the race filled with hate.
History our race is the one tortured and raped.
Love is all we had to give.
All we want is to live.
From the president on down
Our rights burned on crosses and hidden under in justice' rug.
President calls us 'thugs'.
Peaceful protesters around the world, demanding justice for all.
How many more demonstrations' before these evil bricks fall?
Military and law enforcement shooting Rubber bullets, Rubber balls.
President "says start looting, start shooting".
Hateful words he says, then tries to be nice.
Is this the clone of Thomas Dartmouth Rice?

Say things and we are the ones paying the price.
In his tormented soul there is no room for nice.
With all his powerless power I would not want that life.
Slavery, chains, whips, then, now bullets.
Our black babies, Boys, men into the earth their blood splatter.
Seen over the world, in America black lives still do not matter.
When will it end?
President Trump, now tear gas (then water hoses) now officers (then biting dogs)
History repeats itself for us, equality for us 2020…we do not know.
When will they let our roots grow?
Is this the rising of another Jim Crow?
Pushed to the end, taken from the top and placed at the bottom, our faith gives
Us the strength to try.
God will give us our stolen supply.
If not in this life, the next we will live with Him in the sweet by and by.
People around the world praying this beautiful race will not die.
While mothers and relatives of blacks cry.
How can Blacks have a future when our law enforcers keep holding onto the past.
Separate but equal, exchanging white sheets with blue uniforms
And a badge?
Wanting to know why black citizens are outraged and mad.
The world watches America, nodding their heads and sad.
A fruitful land of plenty, not giving the black race any.
Taken from their lands and sold, ancestors worked all their lives, beaten with
Whips and chains, inheritance for their generation a worthless penny.
Knocked down, beaten we get up again.
Bullets targeted at our black Men.
Knocking at equality's door, told we can never come in.
Marching at Washington's gate, our rights we defend.
Characterized as terrorist.
My rights they cannot (don't) comprehend.
Because of my…
Black Skin.

BLACK WIDOW

Whether love, lust or situations connected to my heart, you are my wakened reason.
Brown skin smile like the morning sunrise.
Enticing lips beautiful breast and sensual thighs.
My mirror of hope and its unforeseen lies.
Brief tantalizing moments, path of pleasures, reality I compromised.
I thought if I gave the chambers of my soul only to you.
Possibly in my dreams, there be no other guys.
If asked if I could relive my life with you, truthfully teary eyes.
No hesitation or minute to think…
The only answer…yes in a second's blink.
I was not caught in a web of lies.
Every breath I took with you, into my well answered wishes.
Truth has always greeted me with your unforgettable kisses.
Life, house on a hill is not in our future, nor rocking chairs, holding hands growing old.
I was not blind or mislead, I knew like salad other ingredients added in the bowl.
When I am alone my mind did not wonder, because what we have, when we are apart
Makes this incomplete man whole.
My love for you is all the proof.
We tried to be MR and MRS, we became more distant under the same roof.
Silence was louder than a thunderstorm.

You barely let me hold you in my lonesome arms.
Being in the other room, not able to…did more harm.
Conversations and intimacies did not open its door.
Laughter and its clouds blown away by the winds of time.
You belong to others and I knew you could not be my wife.
Letting go of our pretend home, accepting truth, we embraced beauty beyond the
Waterfalls of life.
Everything is out in the open, from day one.
Wishful thinking daydreaming you would give me a son.
If so, questions is he mine?
It would not have mattered, because he would have come from you my darling love.
My love is for you only, in my heart that is all I see.
I do not care if our bond are roots of polygamy or bigamy?
I give myself to you knowing.
Sun has darken and the moon is saddened, devastating winds blowing.
Death has strangled life's roots from growing.
The windows to heaven are open for me.
I am sadden and thankful holding dear hope, attached pains and misery.
With you has always been where I desire to be.
I hope God has a special place for me.
If possible, from this life into another painfully free.
I will hold onto this one long as I can, until God turns the knob and throws away the key.
My darling your face is all I long to see.
She is wiping the tears from our eyes.
My heart dancing through death's excruciating's pain, smiling and happy.
Holding my hand, kissing my forehead, momentarily I will enter eternity.
My wife she could not be.
I am not blaming her, because I have Aids, no longer HIV.
There were no hidden lies.
She loves me.
I hope God will comfort her when she cries.
Another week cannot be put off for goodbye's.
I am crying deeply inside.

No room for what ifs, buts or why's.

Her smile after today will not be seen through my tearful eyes.

Her beautiful brown skin, she loves me.

Meeting her my lonesome heart changed.

Our love to others seemed complicated and strange.

Asked today if I could relive my life with her, knowing my disease and its overwhelming pain.

Its intense piranha eating burning fiery flame.

Answered…yes, truthfully teary eyes, outcome the same.

Heart full of love, no blame.

Oak tree transformed into a weeping willow.

Head on my pillow.

What we shared only the heavens know.

I wish that more time for us God would let grow.

Looking through the mirror of truth…its time I let go.

Foolishness truth be told it is not so.

Their nonsense gossip asinine man beguiled by…

Black Widow.

BLACK WOMB

Sitting in my room because of COVID-19.

Phase 2, soon they will be re-opening everything.

People coming together because of May 25, 2020, 3 ruthless officers, vicious,

Hateful and fatally mean!

I am mad, angry as hell, to a reoccurring unpunished crime scene!

My restless soul inflamed because truths like these are a black man's daily routines.

Entire Corrupt Judicial system, eyes wide open and will not intervene!

Investigation…Shit, and the facts are in front.

Mirage of justice, broken promises they tease and taunt.

Black wombs, open canal are prey's they hunt!

Wrapped in hate, black lives rolled into a deadly blunt!

Nothings' done, unheard prayers for our daughters and sons!

Reoccurring situations for blacks already foreseen.

Boys in blue, shit on us like a port-o-pot, their God-given latrine.

I am a black man hurting for my race.

Questions in my heart for DR Martin Luther King.

If you were here.

You would see black people are living in a nightmare daily, and not your evaporated dream.

Why white people say, it is not as bad as it seems?

Why don't God hear our cries for justice, instead turn deaf ears to our injustice screams?

I am not questioning your dream, or what you saw for us at the mountain top.

Faith, prayers, and an ocean of tears, your (our) dream 52 years, and mistreatment from them haven't stopped.

Who can we depend on, when in the mirrors face are racists cops?

Justice, freedom taken, pointed fingers and we are the burglar!

Dissected under their microscope regular.

We are not judged by the content of our character.

Breathing black targets, for these hateful predators.

Paragraphs turned into books, written to Supreme court for our equality, Rejected letters!

We know time for us is not getting better.

Their unjust laws, we are not going to settle.

Peace, peace they are killing us like countries in the Middle East.

Through hates eyes we are labeled unworthy, expendable beast.

Their laws, our race will soon cease.

Death for our kind taken, quicker than streaming technology.

Acquittals, blood on their hands,2020 how can this be?

Nothing's changed, blacks still lynched, different methods, same tree.

Not waiting for night fall, no secret building, live streaming… computers, iPhone's TV.

400-500 years forward, and our black race are not free.

Truth it is a façade "Stature of Liberty".

It is for the white man, not for black faces like me.

Opportunity's doorsteps we are pushed a side and kicked.

Countless Emmett Till's they (murder) beat!

Some places in the South we are still not allowed to eat.

In their racists circle, Black's tongue cut out so truth cannot speak.

Freedom, justice for blacks-fables we no longer believe.

Hand cuffed pined on the ground, I cannot breathe.

89-year-old couple sitting on the porch, discussing freedom today… soon we reckoned.

Until 8 minutes and 46 seconds.

Wrinkled shaking hands, unable to make a fist, faith and tears all cried out.

To our ears from his mouth.

Husband replied never!

Down South…

Black man tied to a truck, body parts falling off being dragged by his feet.

Countless bodies thrown in some God-forsaken creek.
Is this the America we want to bring back and keep?
What if the tables were turned and your race we beat?
Today is time for these hateful roots to be burned, no matter how deep.
Into the fire its Confederate flag, monuments, chains, laws let them burn with a firmament
Heat.
Being black you are a victim of police brutality.
We cannot let yesterday's injustices continue to repeat
Death of Black's will not be a merry-go-round of this unjust formality.
Peace, non-violence is what you preached.
DR King, your dream vanishes from our hearts and traveled beyond our reach.
Killing black Men repeatedly, video goes viral, and this teaches...
Its ok racist sucking leeches.
Their asinine heart, God mistake these lower than life, black creatures.
The world watches blacks being beaten and killed, sitting on comfortable bleaches.
Our worth to them, is an out-house full of Shit.
Razors of hate in their truth equality blacks will never get!
Hurricane of violence from them, concussion, broken ribs added to the mix.
Writing the Declaration of Independence... white supremacists?
Treatment before and after 1776?
Band-Aid of lies, it is the same and nothings fixed.
Today white supremacist's uncovered costumes.
Pulled back curtains plotting our day of doom.
Interrogation in the open, no closed-in-room.
Birthed from a black womb, desiring to live, laugh, grow... is that too much to assume?
My future is shortened by my pre-destined white man's tomb
All eyes on us from conception and death's canal,
No tunnel of light, walls of racism and covered clouds of gloom.
One last lethal push...
Dynamite waiting explosive-boom, through a hopeless-
Black Womb.

BROKEN PEBBLES

I gave you laughter and clouds of hope for us.
Trying to break your chambers' walls of distrust.
Holding onto yesteryears hurt and situations you refused to discuss.
Like a well your smiles of fading copper turned to decaying rust.
I was determined to give you mountains of love.
Your heart entwined with decades of lies and all the bad things they placed
In you not allowing good to enter.
Praying God break these unbreakable walls.
My love for you pours from its hopeful waterfalls.
I wish there were a magic potion.
Your hurt is deeper than combined ocean's.
I shower you with fresh bouquets of flowers several times a day.
I call you and send notes saying how beautiful you are.
When someone makes you sad, I will be your kleenex for every tear.
When you feel cold and lonely, I will be your blanket with no expectations.
A genie in your presence, not trapped in a bottle.
Things go wrong, prayers of peace for your mind I will ask God.
Broken pebbles I gave you laughter in clouds of hope for us,
When anger open its door, I will be your mat to step on and kick and punching bag.
When the world hits you, I will stand in front and receive.
If the doctor says you need an organ, I will give you mine.
If I'm not a match, I promise you an organ I will find.
Happiness for you, I will give with every raindrop,

Standing alone knowing you deserve all the joy they took from your beautiful smiles,
You can have mines.
If your arms are too weary for good things, I will give you mines to hold all you think you were not worthy.
When darkness will not let you see the garden, I worked for seasons for you, I will give you my eyes.
Beautiful petals should be waterfalls of peace when the sun goes down and when it rises.
The path of no blackened eyes, broken arms, no view of God's uplifting blue skies, my feet are yours.
Closed doors of simple pleasures in life, my hands I give to you, please open.
Birds singing and the music of peaceful angelic choir's, take my ears and listen.
I want love to cover you like the clouds, and shadows of beauty beyond the waterfalls of life to be the air you breathe.
Sweet honeysuckle 'and gardenia's the aromas of waking with no fear of being hurt anymore.
I have given myself to you completely, within the winds of joy I am free.
Knowing in my loving arms you don't want to be.
I wasn't your knight and shinning armor, but the one who was infected with your misery.
My darling love to prove my undying love, years of hurt in your broken heart, I give you mines that's filled with only true love for its destined donee.
Maybe someday this truth you will see.
Closed doors to hurt, an a second chance of being loved.
I love you, the stone that I once was is now beautiful...Broken pebble's

FORFEITED DIAMOND

Looking across the waters I traveled in my life.
Having everything, houses, jobs supportive wife.
Was not enough, our bond of marriage daily I cut with my selfish knife.
Her tears were like waterfalls that would not stop.
I was too busy desiring the pretty flowers in someone's shop.
I did not see her beauty, daily hurting her was the axe I used to chop.
I was mesmerized by a field of women and refused to water my crop.
Thinking I was God's gift to all the pretty young things.
She knew, never stop being my wife or taking off her wedding ring.
Holding her head up high, being a good wife no matter the heartache I continued to bring.
Wishing I could go back in time and kiss her neck while pushing her on the swing.
My rules and penalties she suffered into her cage she could no longer sing.
This once beautiful swan, now bruised, broken too afraid to stretch her wings.
Her smile covers her hurting heart holding my hand, sitting by her unfaithful king.
I was the one who cut a beautiful thriving spread into tiny pieces of a dying string.
Love seldom came from my heart to her, mostly erupting volcanoes of mean.
Much love and patience she continued to find hope in a dying stream.
I did not care, to the table and bedroom I bought and gave nothing.
Her soaked pillow she held onto along with her dreams.

Talking to me saying loving you and marriage was our choice.
I would get a pillow and blanket, headed for the couch, my infidelities no remorse.
Question, who was that gentle soul who came riding upon a disappearing horse.
His charm and smile wakened by his caring voice.
Tender loving words now anger and hate pours from his heart and mouth'
Entwined with each other then, now in the same house, further than the North and South.
What has happened, that you allowed darkness to follow?
Ground of truth no longer full but hollow.
Your enemies you call friend their lies you know and still swallow.
Anger you say because of me is the reason you turned to the bottle.
Our simple life was too complicated, I did nothing wrong my love you reject.
I do not understand, in your eyes I used to be the sunrise now a fading speck.
All your infidelity's, hopeful prayers and blackened eyes and twisted arms I get?
I have given you unconditional love and respect.
Sun is shining and my heart is black and not rainbow shades of blue.
Through it all my prayers were good things for you.
Late night meetings and the weekends you party.
Living like you were single, a man whose 18 or 20 not realizing you are 40.
Your dinner was always prepared,
Even though home you were never there.
Clothes always washed and ironed.
Things didn't go as planned; you'd ripped me like a lion.
I get bitter words; she gets roses and a bottle of wine.
Forgive him Lord he is broken and blind.
Seeds you refuse to share with me,
Outside kids I think it is 3.
Francis, Carl, and Little Bobbie.
This is all I have to give a hug continued prayers and your wedding ring.
50 years and God answered my prayers, He's the only one in my life I am willing to share.

I do not hate you Bobbie; hand to God I swear.
Trust in God, when everything fails, He will always be there.
Forgive me came from my lips and from hers a goodbye kiss
A forfeited diamond upon its weary walls I daily pissed.
Dying dreams, pushed plans and broken wrist.
In heaven my name was omitted from its list.
Sitting here my life flashes before me, good things from her, twisted arms, and blackened eyes
I punched with my fist.
Watching her walk away, Lord knows a Forfeited Diamond I am going to truly miss.
I was the king on top of the hill.
Seldom came home to nightly prepared meals.
I gnoring my queen into her life, shame and licks I drilled.
I know she was ok, because I paid the bills.
Her days of laughter and sunshine were blocked by darkness and hatred.
I was a fisherman and women I caught on my reel.
Marriage did not matter, being faithful was not in the deal.
My faithful jewel her joy I killed.
My unfaithfulness into our marriage repeatedly I spilled.
I never doubted her love or thought the day would come for me when she would not be there.
My forfeited diamond is gone because I was a foolish selfish person who did not care.
Women every day of the week, I was a player.
Reaping what I have sown now I meet my life's slayer.
70 years old, money women and alone.
My so-called friends, and jobs all gone.
3 kids I barely know will be taken care of until grown.
Cannot care for self, my forfeited diamond put me in a nursing home.
She gave love to me and I treated her wrong?
Baby mamas' saw dollars then, now with other men, having moved on.
My forfeited diamond that I beat daily, thought was fragile and weak is strong.
Tears from me she refuses to remain in my mansion or sit on a dying throne.

Too many years in that place, trying to fit in and never belong.

My forfeited diamond, I threw away 50 some years and today I recognize.

Tears for me a hug, wedding ring, and goodbye kiss, she really did care.

Tears, tears MR Bobbie, it is time for bingo, do you need help with your wheelchair?

Forfeited Diamond

GOLDEN YEARS

Kids playing in the back yard, hearts filled with laughter.

Schools days your girlfriends and the situations after.

Sitting on our pretend bench, watching the sun rise.

You were gifted with talents; I saw underneath your petals of love.

When those mean girls picked with me and pushing me down, you picked me up.

Books thrown on the floor.

Tears of joy because when I picked them up, not seeing you, I felt your presence.

In your eyes I was not an ugly duckling.

Through my many storms, I was ok, because there was a letter from you in my mailbox.

God do not allow more than we can endure.

Open blinded eyes and see.

Your continual words of encouragement, I am unique…there is no other like me.

Lunch time I set in the corner, you would get my plate and I set in the center.

I knew I was plain, not like the other girls, so in your eyes I would never be.

In my world I pretended being your wife.

Your kindness was beyond the waterfalls of life.

You were always in my heart's chambers.

Silent prayers I wondered if God answered?

Health problems, wrinkled hands, arthritis, foreclosure, children, grandbabies, weddings… He did.

Holding your hand for real, head on your shoulder.

Seeds of wisdom blossom as we grew older.

Loving me form the first day you saw me playing in the back yard.

I was pretending with them, wanting to be with you.

Knowing it was wrong, but I wanted those girls to be mean; so, I could come to your rescue.

I am sorry for the many tears on your pillow.

You waited for me untainted.

I was the ugly duckling, sleeping with all those girls.

I was foolish, fulfilling my lustful needs.

I give thanks to God for kept seeds.

No life amongst sinful weeds.

You are so beautiful, I love you.

Years of this and that you remained faithful?

Sitting on a bench, watching the sun rise.

The heavens smile and winds cries...

"This is the beginning of our precious lives."

At the doctor's office a man said I am 75, and it is supposed to be my golden years, old sick,

Dying, what is golden about that?

We looked at each other and smiled because wisdom taught us, that sharing our lives through

Everything and having a peaceful mind, and God's unconditional love is what makes our lives

Golden years, having had the pleasure of God's kindness, family, friends, jobs nice home.

Was not so much as golden years, but given the blessing to enjoy these years and knowing we

Did not deserve one golden day given.

All the years that lay ahead for us to embrace and endure.

Thank you, Father God.

We are blessed with 65 years with the person You knew would prolong each other's life.

My darling husband, and my beautiful wife.

HOLLOW

be a good man and do the right thing always; and do not let seldom be a
temporarily elevator escaping to do wrong.
life is hard and nothing is given, a man has many definitions when it comes
to you my darken son, do not listen to their lies.
truths I ate daily even when my belly was empty. my parents teaching was
embedded in the halls, sky piecing roof and every corner in our crumbling
home.
it is love and faith is what made it to withstand every storm.
the cold winters covered shadow was there after its season was gone.
the saying is true I could not hurt a fly or break a creature's bone.
man is a creature himself, no matter the soil he was grown.
there is a beast inside of us all regardless the path we are on.
kneeling by and old oak tree (parent's grave), they are gone.
my path, their teachings of faith and love keeps me strong.
tears embracing flowers I place on their tombstone.
father and mother, I will not get on the elevator of wrong.
you are in the earth beneath and the heaven's rain is a beautiful uplifting
song.
thanking God for my blessings from above.
growing up hate and darkness could not block my parents shield of love.
the world said I could not, my faith said I can.
told love is not the answer to life, too young but in time I would understand.
many roads I wanted to travel becoming a man.
book of truth my bible God has a plan.
pushed and shoved in anger I refused to hit another with my fist,

thinking I was on the right path, being told enlist.
maybe just maybe my calling is this?
on injustice walls for all I will piss.
I know this is the right thing for me.
be all that my country wants me to be.
the hidden truth of it all I could not see.
my difficulties became victories.
every medal of honor I achieved.
20 years I gave and did not want to leave.
the humble person I was have been transformed into an aggressive trouble man.
Not the little boy who cried because the wind took his kite.
I am my own man not worried about being stabbed in the heart with hatred's knife.
married to my God-given duty, no need for kids or wife.
Before….
I was living "Beauty Beyond the Waterfalls of Life".
I would not hurt a fly...
several baths during the day blood on my hands, if mother were alive, she'd cry.
men women and children…people in general did they have to die?
rollercoaster screams, hidden truths covered with a lie.
Souls taken within a blink of an eye.
Nightmares, daydreams are clouds of darkness, cannot separate no matter how hard I try.
Squeezing my forehead, who am I?
Suffering, teeth of pain and its ugliness, winds sings you are not going to die.
Head on my pillow of death's antagonizing hatred, no breath of relief.
There is no hope for me but endure my destined grief.
Time choke my soul allow death's mouth to kiss.
Please swallow me quickly within your abyss.
Upon my darken wall-soul let acid piss!
Death is torturing me like long suffering terminal cancer.
I became who they wanted me to be, I can be no other...love is not the answer.

Truth be told with us all is an unknown beast.

Blood on my hands cannot be pardon by the world's highest priest.

My parents kneading ingredients of love and faith, died when I was stationed in the Middle East.

So much for believing in world peace.

Today I am decorated like a Xmas tree.

The thing I am I no loner wish to be.

This is me and in the mirrors of my soul I can never flee...

Who was the enemy?

No smile on my face, days, and nights much misery.

Medals stacked in a pile.

Desiring to go back in time being cuddled in my mother's arms when I was a Child,

20 years of this begging to vanish from this never-ending trial.

Tears and an ocean of innocent blood have washed away my smile.

Handshakes, congratulations, we are proud and thanks for your service, locked within no end of freedom.

Momma I am sorry, back then I meant every word.

Would not kill a fly, definitely not a bird.

Listening to others definition.

Parents teaching of love, could not be heard.

On the other side of the rainbow waiting for me is quicksand and mud.

Upon my head are clouds of raindrops turned into cries of innocent blood.

Daily I pray God let me drown, please stop this reoccurring flood.

A child filled with love and hope.

On another path being hung with my own hand-held rope.

Medications, therapy, and ingredients added in the pot.

My torment is not going to stop!

A life with meaning is no more, their path of darkness I followed.

Its pills I continue to swallow.

Honored and praised today in a room filled with people.

I stand alone no longer full of love and life.

Guilty, overwhelmed, lost...

Hollow

IF MY LIFE WERE MY DREAMS

A beautiful black hollyhock standing under a streetlight, feather umbrella
Held in her silky kissable hands.
Tantalizing smile could brighten miles of deserted miserable land.
I glance for a second, tight fitting gown unraveling every strand.
Intimacy's with her comes with a price, and I am not that man.
On the elevator of wrong (5th floor) lips, breast, I do not think I can.
Supermarket, school, church minding me, vultures like razors in the sand.
Their false charm are death's blades to my life-cutting fan.
Behind their smiles' façade are deceits' lethal documented plan.
Lusciously lips web of lies do not fall into their sinful quicksand.
I will have no part with them, their worth is more, trying to explain they
do not understand.
Youth is temporarily and true beauty never grows old.
Wrinkles will blanket your skin, plump breast will sag, and your petals
will fold.
I will be the patient gentleman who sees a shining diamond ◊ and windows
of gold.
Hoping into your heart you will let me hold.
Into our garden, God lets us stroll.
I see your true beauty, your inner soul.
God made women more beautiful than flowers and sweeter than dewberries.
More delectable than virgin strawberries.
God gave women an amazing sacred garden.
Sadly, allowing continued abuse of its passion fruits has become an
unwanted cemetery.

Their uniqueness and petals of life, once amazing are plain simple ordinary.
Self-respect, value, more lies underneath a tombstone in its public shameful library.
Reasons do not matter, because in their rainbow blackness and hopelessness written in her dictionary.
If only she could find a magical wand or make-believe god fairy.
Hollow prayers, too much time given to undeserving ones, heavens will I marry?
Crossed fingers hoping across the threshold her groom will someday carry.
Broken mirrors, shattered glass.
Haunted by pleasures in her past.
My once beautiful garden of hope is now thorns and thistles,
weeds and its mountains of trash.
Too late for second chances, mind tired, body broken.
Apologies from my desert lips will never be heard or spoken.
I was a fool to believe I was every man's God-given token.
Perfect lips body and my voice sweeter than honey.
My world of pleasures men could not resist, indulging in every fantasy.
Was I living in the moments of my façade's insanity?
Kisses, caresses being loved by so many romantically.
I gave them waterfalls of intimacy.
Love was not present, lustful penetrating moments combined anatomy.
Rising in the arms of different faces, taken in the clouds' sensual gravity.
Sun goes to sleep; I am awaken by pulsating's heartbeats erratically.
Held by many souls in my world fact or enchantingly.
Except one, my darling simple Anthony.
Life has a way of opening portals that you must see.
Beauty is who I am to be.
Life, time getting older isn't the path for me.
Don Perignon in my glass, dissolving pills, memories of pleasures.
I have loved so many, I am every hurting man's remedy.
I have given complete ecstasies'.
Covered raincoats and no accountable disease.
Goddess worshipped and praised on thankful knees.
In my dreams I am free.

Times' door is shut and its wrinkles, body aches and ugliness has vanished in the sea.

I will embrace beauty beyond the waterfalls of life, its triumph, and no tragedies.

If awaken and replaced mirrors of truth, shadows of vanity.

Glass of Dom Perignon, dissolved pills, the other side of my true destiny.

Wrinkles, age spots, eyeglasses will never be my identity.

Handheld guided by death's mortality.

Smothered by me if my end is vanity let me die instantly!

Into the mirror of old age, I defy I scream!

One last sincere request to the heavens so it seems.

Only…

If my life were my dreams?

LIFE A VAPOR

I was not the best mom and I am still not, and I realize I have to let them go.
I am tired of it all, my heart is hurting because I have held them to long and maybe
Crippled their I cans, I am sorry, prayers for a miracle that is beyond my reach. Maybe
God is saying, shame on me for letting go of His hand. I do not know if this mountain is
Going to get bigger or crumble. I wish I could go back with my head on my mom's lap.
Hoping for petals of my birth to never happened, my tears are like waterfall's that's
Destiny and my feet are so tired of this never-ending path that I have been on with no rays of sunshine.
My future tears of joy given to someone more deserving. My love for God is not what it used
To be, I am tired of being the answer when I am truly the problem life like a vapor, I cannot go back anymore
I do not want to go on, tears tears wash me away in the ocean of no return. Why am I still here?
Pity's closed its door telling me it is full. Happiness sings for others and having no vacancy
For me, clouds of laughter the world embraces, the little lost black girl covered with make-up. Pretending

Not wanting darkness to be the shadow her hurting body was born believing foolish fables…she was cursed.

Her mind so full of things, she cannot see her petals are amaziningly more beautiful than all the darkness her eyes

Only sees. Hands thrown in the air my heart wishes for amnesia to fill its chambers. Unwritten documents no ss-card or

Birth certificate leading a trail to her…life a vapor, no worries of having to walk this path or take this hurtful journey…no more tears of a foundation of what the winds blew over her disappearing shadow filled with why's and questions who am I, it's door of rain drops of eternal peace now opens for me today that vapor of life sets my overwhelming tears free. My heart into the winds' clouds of joy covers me, it is time God opens the doors and welcomes me.

MOTHER'S NOTES

Pretending I am on TV, bigger than life.
My favorite watching the elite, famous people on the red-carpet.
Knowing one day I will be.
Memories of sitting on the floor watching TV as a child.
Mom and dad on couch, sitcoms that made them smile.
She would sing the Love Boat come aboard,
Looking at daddy, a trip they could not afford.
Saturday evening, I let them enjoy TV alone.
She would sing and not miss a word to the song.
After given my inner gold.
I vowed that they would take a cruise, if not on the Pacific Princess.
I would save money from different jobs.
Mowing lawns, washing cars, building fences.
Time's hand on the clock, I came to my senses
This chain link for me is too extensive.
That kind of work gets you here, standing grounds of pretenses.
I have no doubt, I am going to go higher than the clouds.
The world will shout praises to me aloud.
I wanted so much for her, more than dad.
She would say be content, you will never have it all.
I know you from the first kick in my belly, and at seven months when you
crawled.
Knowing she was the petals that showered dad when trapped
Between brick walls.
Tending to the house and her peaceful garden, and my many

Bruises and countless falls.
When bullied at school it was her who I called.
Holding my head in her lap, and her tears washing away
Hurtful words that made me feel small.
From that day forward, I was not bullied because it Hurt her more than me
And that Hurt me too much.
Those bullies kept bullying me till I was grown.
Son it seems harder to do right and easier doing wrong.
Not so.
Sometimes I think she knew me more than myself.
Mom never knew, her beautiful soft petals made her little boy strong
We did not tell dad because I told her they left me alone.
Every other Saturday I am between mom and dad on the couch, singing
The lyrics to the Love Boat song.
Lay's potato chips, ham, and cheese sandwhiches, and fruit punch.
That was tomorrow's lunch.
Hot days headed to school and from, mom sitting on the steps.
Drinking the rest of my lemonade.
Kiss me on my forehead, saying son fists do not make a man brave.
Do the right thing always and behave.
In my pocket another note she gave.
I made it to the top having more than enough.
Dad did not stop working and mom petals remained soft.
I made it on top of the clouds.
Dad became angry cold-hearted and tough.
I gave them everything I could think of because life was not easy but
rough.
I gave her a mansion with a big kitchen, back yard, she could have the
Biggest garden and people to tend to it.
Having tools that dad did not have to fix, to fix.
Dad had 2 big red trucks, and a pond he could go fishing anytime.
Did not have to be at work before the dawn and coming home past nine.
I did not understand.
Mom, I want to give you both the world.
She kissed my forehead and said,
Sitting on the front porch steps, drinking the rest of your lemonade

Pushing you on a swing, planting fruits and vegetables in my little garden.
Your dad going to work at dawn and coming home after dark.
Sitting in front of the TV that is our world.
We do not need a mansion with rooms we will never fill, vehicles when we can only drive
One at a time.
That old creek beats any pond that is made in a few hours no matter how deep.
The land we have; your mansion cannot sit.
Our lives could never fit.
The pond that is surrounded by a golf course, and tropical fish.
I do not need pure silverware and coated diamonds in my eating dish.
Son, we did not raise you like this.
Our land is handed down through generations if we sold it for any
Reasons, on our family tree we piss.
I am not fussing at you, we want you to understand, blood sweat, deaths,
Paying triple for our land our feet and knees into the earth our muscles twist.
Born in Poverty is not a curse, nor darkness.
Times of struggle's for our people, with thankfulness we reminisce.
The lives taken their tears of growth we kiss.
We would not want anything different, no matter if granted any wish.
To not have the little you see, our lives we would gladly dismiss.
Our ancestors trail of tears, failures, triumphant, faith we would not exist.
What you cannot or do not see are grounds of hope and not some darkened abyss.
If only you could imagine touchable rainbows and beautiful waterfalls, maybe
You would see our land is silver linings of this.
We do not need the world because this birthright is more than the world.
Son, for you and all the others who have these bigger than big mansion, it
Would be filled with doubt, and betrayal, no amount of money can make
You feel that secure in something that huge.
Money buys things and also people, the old is no different than new.
Be careful, this game is eternal, Satan do not play fair.
I am not saying it is wrong to be rich and have houses and land.

If wrong doings is how to hold onto it, that is not right.
When our ancestors had to endure so much for us to have a inch of our
Taken land, equality, and our precious lives.
We do not want you to be blinded by vanity,
Nor others puppet on strings, climbing to the top, when you have fallen
To the bottom of greed's well.
We love you, and if you decide to remain, our love will not change.
If there was a hidden camera in these mansions, loneliness' would be its
lens.
Covered with darkness that dwells within.
The people who work for you are your employees, not friends'.
Blinded, you cannot see vanity's façade and its lethal sin.
Vanities vanities, your inner gold is more.
You have accomplished all you set out to do, we are proud, so very proud.
Be content son, stop reaching for the moon and stars.
Your inner gold, you are more precious than mansions, fame, garage filled
with cars.
My son, my notes to you are my tears hoping you do not get trapped within
vanity's bars.
I know you, not giving up.
When God made you, He did not make a carbon copy, you are unique.
That should be enough. Your Father have many mansions, sickness, pain
Loneliness, darkness can never enter, if we endure down here under the
moon
Stars and its mountains of trials and multiple falls, knowing to get up.
God has a place for His children, tried by and through the fire, you will
come out
As pure gold.
Pride and greed is like the ocean it is never full.
You entertain people over the world, neither of you know the other.
Your bank account is probably bigger than my mind can grasp.
No amount of money should change a good person inside.
If you are…
Fame and fortune, usually God is not included, when darkness comes
It will entertain you with its buffet of false hope, love, and stability.
Look around we have peace here, the higher you go up fame's ladder

The eviler you'll do to keep it; your beautiful God-given soul will eventually die.

We do not want to see your death broadcast on TV, drug overdose, or whatever

Lies they tell to get ratings, only God will know the truth and your riches.

Puppets on Satan's strings, soul-less phonies'

We do not want any part. We will not be attending any ceremonies.

The $20.000 dress and overpriced shoes and jewelry, along with

Tuxedo and accessories for your dad, take them back. We do not want them.

If you do get a Grammy, Emmy, Oscar or whatever, I hope you remember the notes

I placed in your pocket, daily, throughout high school. sitting on the porch drinking lemonade. Three years later, he is placing flowers on his parents grave.

Tears and prayers wasn't enough to keep their son' soul saved.

Notes he kept from his school years, looking back

Mom on the steps drinking his half of the lemonade.

The notes she gave him were engraved on his parent's tombstone

God grant me the serenity to accept the things I cannot change, courage to change

The things I can, and wisdom to know the difference...

Remember my son, their world and ours' do not entwine, because darkness hate light

We hope and pray God's light do not go out in you.

Please do not hardened your heart like Pharaoh.

More important, God wants you to walk the straight and narrow.

It is the color of truth.

We know who you are and love you anyway son.

Years of hopeful notes to weaken your oceans of greed, only hardened the inner you.

Kneeling at their graveside the wind whispers into his ears she knew.

MY LOVE

2 afraid 2 let go of yesterday and its lies of happiness 4 us.

I forgive you against broken mirrors of trust.

My insecurities and mood swings, through counseling I will adjust.

When you do not return my calls, I promise to be patient and not fuss.

Whatever walls or barricades, together tearing them down.

You are the only one in my heart.

I know you love me.

I promise to always be true.

I will try not to smother you with my love.

Understanding will be the door I open daily.

And patience's knob will let me in.

When life is overwhelming, I will be your punching bag if needed.

The darkness that is inside of you, I will be your IV, a disposable drain.

I love you and do not want to be the source of your hurting pain.

If more time is what you need, understanding's door, I will open and not complain.

I will be your blanket to keep you warm, an umbrella from getting soaked in the rain.

If you are ashamed of me, I will let you be in the front and I will be hidden in the back.

When it comes to you, I am your soldier one hundred percent dedicated.

Soothing instruments and gentle waves will be peaceful music when your life seems complicated.

Time will heal your broken promises and my hopeful prayers.

Clouds gathering my tear drops for brighter joys ahead.

I love you deeply. My ocean of tears and unanswered prayers will be answered one day.

The petals of our love will be mutual. The world whispers I am a fool,

Not understanding my thoughts, dreams and holding onto someone, whose letting me go.

I refuse to believe there is no hope in a black rose.

I look beyond its outer beauty of death and see waterfalls of thriving petals of life.

Fool is not who I am, I was thirsty, and he was the well that let me drink.

In my shoes or not, that desert afternoon kindness open its door.

I refuse to drink from another well, only his.

I see others drink from your well, my heart knows in the future his will be dry.

That day I will be the well that soothes your thirst, and your heart will open its door to me only.

My love for him goes much deeper, than all those who he shares it with.

The sun shines, wind blows and soon his head will lay next to mine on my thankful teary pillow.

If the world could x-ray the roots of my love, it is dimensions of life with no ending.

I love him.

I know she has a place in your heart.

God, I ask, give me a tiny corner, or speck within your chambers.

I love you.

Time I will give you because that is what is needed.

Teary pillow of truth I believe you will let go of her.

Its treasure chest I open, only to find its filled with unending lies.

I forgive you from the moon going down and morning sunrise.

Kissing my breast and caressing my thighs.

I was pure, untouched until you opened my petals

Making love to me out of body experience, intimacy, sexually mesmerized.

Rainbows of exploding ecstasies'.

Heart racing, body trembling, pleasures consistently.

That desert day I memorized.

Years from now, sight going dim, in my heart like that afternoon I will visualize.

We became one, the scales of never being loved fell from my heart and teary eyes.

Thanking the heaven's for you.

Love I never thought its door would open to me.

That desert afternoon,

Loving me may have been a cool breeze to you.

You did the impossible, allowing closed petals to being loved.

Loneliness', and its shadow are buried.

In the heavens our love the angels carries.

I gave myself to my love, someday soon he will give himself to me only.

My love is enough for the both of us.

It has been 30 years and hope is like a beautiful black rose.

Its ending and beginning is the same door called patient.

I love you my love, you are my ending and my beginning.

I will wait an eternity to be held in your unforgettable arms, and to lay

My heart next to yours and listen to a heavenly choir.

I know you do not love me the same, it do not matter because you

Released me from hell's loneliness and its tormenting chains.

I thank you for a taste of heaven and its rainbows' of temporarily kindness

From your tender lips of pleasures and filling my desert lips with windowpanes of love.

NOTHING'S CHANGED

It is what it was and remains
You say look at the clock, time has changed.
True, different whips same controllers in the game.
Called nigger, instead my God-given name.
One of the tribes of Judah.
Removed from our ankles necks and wrists.
Justice like the wind I cannot touch cannot kiss.
Our lives do not matter, against the walls our rights daily you piss.
Life's ring being punched daily with your wicked fist.
Equality justice our names never added to your list.
???... Did God give you ALL the land?
Broken backs, steps you continue to stand.
This system characterize us lower than a dog, definitely not a man.
We are the problem you try to contain.
Nothing is changed…
Pointed fingers blacks, poverty, drugs, injustices, guns
Will you tell us where it all came from?
Legally…we are the Targets your bullets aim?
Nothings done…2020 what a shame.
In the mirror of truth, you are the blame.

PAINTED FLOOR

There once was a girl… a diamond in the rough some would say.

She smiled so bright, her laughter. oh, her laughter was as a sweet yet bitter song.

She imagined a world where she could be alone yet not lonely.

Her reality consuming her, darkness began to overtake her.

No one understood why this once joyful young lady became her own destruction.

No one cared to understand.

And she did not care for anyone too.

For she knew no one could save her from the lover she knew.

No one could love her beyond the love she only knew.

And no one could replace the false love she chased.

That once beautiful smile faded every time, she hit the floor.

That once sweet laughter turned to hidden tears of pain.

As her blood stained.

Feeling guilt, feeling shame, feeling death yet it never came.

Another night left lonely only to clean her paint off the floors.

Growing tiresome she can endure no more for she was so much more.

now being lowered beneath the dust. Silence befalls us.

You wonder who she is… who she once was… you need not to look any further.

For she is the tears beneath your own eyes.

She is hidden the pain you try to hide.

The fear of tomorrow, she is…

She is you… She is me… Yet WE SURVIVED!!!

PETALS OF INSANITY

Wind blowing through the forest, I am released from my shell.
Furious unforeseen forces, pushed me to the bottom of ceiba's - trees
Questions of my destined hell.
Frightened I cannot see beauty, only the fading mountain I fell.
Alive or not, panicked voice not heard, because I am in the heart of the
Earth, the depths' has silenced my yell.
Broken tombstones, mirrorless shadows' of blackness is this the
Bottomless pit I am to dwell?
If I had a rifle, aimed toward me, kissing its barrel before being fired, I
would embrace its smell.
There is no need to live, running having no feet, yet I am compelled.
Vague memories of a faceless picture frame.
Trapped because of ignorance, mostly pride, the heaven's I blame.
Preachers, pastors, men of God. Stealing, lying having no shame.
Your rod of chastisement, for me You aim?
I am not the wolf pretending to be a sheep, in Your name.
I am being punished with Your internal flame.
Your peaceful present told to depart.
Am I invisible, or not even present in the earth's heart?
This horrible manuscript or movie, and I am the puppet to play the part.
Collecting falling seashells, to try and understand pieces of this
Confusing puzzle to my spirit's ending or beginning.
My tears are many wells gone dry.
Solicitor, I must have been because bitterness, discomfort and torment
is my

Heavenly supply.

Its clouds are not white, blue is now oceans of deserted sky.

The roots of my justice lingers on, no intentions for me to die.

Scorched scales, no silver linings, not knowing time I try.

Who am I?

The offspring of deadvlei?

Praying for peaceful views from this point of life, I think not.

My uncovered truth has been seen,

The deadly truth of who I am.

Foolish soul questioning everything, chained locked and eternally dammed.

I thought I was bigger than this so-called God.

Reasons of my darkened life tragedies.

Dim light took me to the door, investigating portal of curiosity.

Warnings along its path, I refused to see.

My encyclopedia of doubt, entering realm that was not for me.

Boldly entering dimensions my ignorance, exchanged soul sacrificed by stupidity.

Burning flames mountain of lies, locked chains, no key.

Heaven, hell, purgatory, God, devil, good, bad, real, fake path to insanity.

Answers, questions, puzzles, am I the enemy?

Bondage, wealth, we are all shades of cursed poverty.

Sacrificing on paths destined to the top, open doors to misery.

Feet on solid ground, mind full heartbroken ingredients, façade of false prosperity.

Past decisions are present day imprisonment of never being free.

Forming man from the ground, breathing being, how can this be?

My days nights are the same, living dying amongst the roots of a tree.

Your loving warning's I refused to see.

Truth, soul given in exchanged for worldly vanity.

I refuse to admit If I was wrong,

Because I did not asked to be here or there.

I did not ask to have atheist parents, who did not believe in Christianity.

My quest has ended its search for true humanity.

Fear surrounds me like a hunted animal in the South African Safari.

No more calming nights, enjoying twinkling lights so amaziningly starry.

My soul is entwined with scorpions' venom and its roots deeper than a pallial marri.
Like Adam You gave me my parents.
You banned me from being in Your glory.
So, from my transparent soul, I'm not sorry.
If this is my due punishment, please hurry.

REHAB FOR ME

Staring at the hands on the clock my heart looks over our life.
I am learning.
In the beginning it was fun, did not think I would be your wife.
Laughter and hopeful dreams open its door.
Because of you that little abused girl's shadow was not following me anymore.
Waterfalls, rising of the sun, winds singing peaceful melodies.
In my past relationships lies licks and never-ending infidelities.
Robert, I want to run with you in a field of beautiful flowers.
I want your arms to hold me tight, dancing in the midnight showers.
Being loved by you, breaking my walls of hurt like mountains of breath-taking melting snow.
Happiness and its rainbows falling clouds covering us within its shadow.
In our garden my bruises and disappointments will not grow.
Prayers and nurturing my heart like a caring farmer.
Did not know you were my knight and shining armor.
We had our share of life and its dark clouds.
I am sorry because some of your tears was me and I am not proud.
My knight who was always there to make me smile.
I am lost looking for you, like a motherless child.
Those three tender words from me to you…boy, it has been awhile.
Our life flashes before my eyes.
I am praying that God brings back blue skies.
You are one of the good guys.

My life with you are waterfalls of healing with every fallen tear my heart
cries.
In the corner praying the angels anoint your body in ICU.
Our lives a beautiful bond, not knowing what to do.
Tears falling from my heart into my eyes, sadden and blue.
God, please let Robert make it through.
I know sometimes I was unforgiving childish and mean.
Our life and I am sorry for multiple petty things.
I want Robert to live and not be on a breathing machine.
His body is weak and mind not knowing he is alive.
Mouth taped; tubes more than I want to see.
By my side is where I want Robert to be.
Death's strings, right now in Your precious name untie.
Fill our hopeful well that was dry.
Lord make him better, do not let him die.
Tests after test the finding negative, he lay there like he is gone.
God please, please tell death's angel to leave him alone.
I am holding his hand, praying sincerely my faith is strong.
Lord please let Your will be for him to come home.
Looking at him lying there... into the mirror I see my faults.
Should have given him love, because into my heart that is what he brought.
Could haves and should haves, into his wounds I poured angry salt.
Lord I love him please let him live.
He is the one in the hospital and I am the one being operated on.
Lord, I will not complain when I have to prepare his meals.
The doctor says he will have to learn motor skills.
That is a blessing by his side down or up life's roughed hills.
In our garden of life laughter his spirit gives.
Praying Father today on this bridge health and strength are within each
brick You build.
Robert coming home, Father I know it is Your will.
Right now, my husband is healed.
Robert will learn to speak, and I will learn to listen.
He will learn to sit, and I will learn to kneel and pray.

He will learn to use his arms and I will learn to hold him often.
He will learn to walk, and I will learn to be by his side.
Thank You God.
together with my husband and I will be the learning student.

ROOTS OF PRIDE

Smog and its oceans of pollution its poisons into my choking lungs being filled.

City life was too much, so I moved and built my castle on top of a country hill.

The sun would pierce through and the heavens' dewdrop tears dripping from my windowsill.

Fragrances of fruits vegetables and sweet flowers' petals waking in a non-chemical field.

Walking to the pond, sugarcane pole, no fancy fishing reel.

Barefoot on a dirt road bucket in one hand fetching todays meal.

Breathing country air its non-pesticides potatoes and onions I peel.

Neighbors miles away, not so close when you open your window, their presence you see and feel.

TV news daily surplus of guns innocent people getting killed.

Politicians, policemen, judges desiring greed its corruption into the street's spills.

Doctors, priest, preachers, congress, illuminati they are part of the deal.

I had to get away eat food that is not genetically modified but real.

It was too busy no time to breathe, enjoy the waves or sunrise on a ship that is sure to sink.

Business, parties, meetings around the clock, a pill for everything, speak, sleep eat drink.

Merry-go-round, puppet on a string out-of-body experience I cannot think.

Eyes open wide living in a circle of darkness, do not know if the paintings yellow green or pink?

Robes red, black, white, gray candles cup of blood whose do not know, pores of my skin itch and stink.

House on a hill green grass my feet cannot feel, fresh air gone in a wink.

I had it all ...gone in a selfish blink.

Praying for rows of peace hoping the clouds sprinkle.

What is happening, am I the brother of Rip Van Winkle?

Alone sitting in the boardroom body soaking wet.

Phone rings...

About to land, cannot be I am afraid of height and I do not own a jet.

No, where am I, what meeting, looking out the window I forget.

Cup of blood, rituals burned candles riches everything planned and set.

Hour of darkness, mind twisted Lord not yet?

Apologies for my sins, my soul traded in a losing bet.

I am sorry Lord and this evil I have done; I sincerely regret.

Where am I?

Starring at people who I never met.

Stop breathe relax...

God, no it is clear as a fax.

The life I had, did not want, and cannot get back.

The sun and its rays are not blue but eternal clouds of black.

Bridges burned; hope thrown in a volcano because riches I desired alone life' tracks.

House on a hill was a two-room shack.

Wanting more than fields of fruits vegetables and not enough in my empty sack.

Caring for rows in a field, away with a sling blade I hacked!

City life my heart desired, sold the land.

I am not my grandparents or parents I wanted more, if alive they would not understand.

In the world out there I can be, farming is not my plan.

Ghost town humph, away from it I ran.

Bare foot, pig feeding, jean patched, chopping wood I cannot be a man.

I am not dreaming; this pump my hands will no longer prime.

Satan when you got it all, now it is time.

Into your overflowing basket your soul is mines'.

That shack on top of the hill was treasure's your greedy heart did not need to find.

You wanted more and more, until the simple pleasures in life you left behind.

You had everything, reaching for facades of this you became blind.

I gave you what you asked, the proof look at your signature in blood you signed.

What will it be jump out a window...

Overdose, shoot yourself, make sure you leave a note.

Let's not go down that road, you know I am a liar.

One thing for sure we both are going to burn in the lake of fire.

Boy the souls you brought to me on hell's wall, will be a picture of the fool most admired.

Your time has expired!

What is your pleasure, I gave you whatsoever you desired.

THE FATHER ASKS SATAN

From the beginning of time have I not showered you with love and My Holy Spirit Divine? Have I not let you sparkle and shine? Was there a moment I treated you unkind?

Have I not made you the highest angel, give you a voice like no other? Have I not treated you like a son and loving brother?

Have I given you more than you could not take? The more I gave you, your love weakened, jealousy and pride into your soul brought forth darkness and hate.

I knew you before you were. I never trivialized you, swore at you, making you feel useless, or small.

Have I not lead the path of truth for you always, narrow, and straight?

There were no misunderstandings between us. I gave you love, you could and did for a little time relate.

You were cast from heaven and banned never to enter its holy gates. A third of heaven's angels with you. A good leader you could have been,

But you rejected my commandments and embraced sin.

Was I not a loving Father and caring friend?

You was safe from harm in My holy paradise, you rejected Me and My unconditional love, did not think twice.

Death you brought on mankind. I having to let My Son come down and be the only worthy sacrifice.

You were more than a thorn in myside. My Son on a tree He hung and died. I know in My shadow you could not abide.

You are filled with wickedness and evil, your continual disgust with Me and your selfish pride, not to mention you are the father of lies.

There is no hope in you, we both know I tried.

Did you not know I knew the real you from within your darkened soul? No vessel and expiring empty hole.

For you to say bow to me I give you...? No, you cannot. Being Me and having My kingdom is a myth, a reality only in your make-believe dreams. I was just and loving, you are filled with wickedness and schemes. I showered you with righteousness, love, love, and love and I am the One you did not trust.

The day will come when you bow to Me saying "LORD OF LORDS AND KING OF KINGS" FAITHFUL TRUE AND JUST"!

Your destiny in the lake of fire is a necessity, a definite must. Let Me finish talking, hush!

Deceive the world but those that are mine you cannot take from My hands. Thou fool, all you set out to do, you think your wicked kingdom will rule the land, like Pharaoh's hardened heart caused the plague's. Your ending was not My desire,

But your eternal death is in the lake of fire!

THESE THINGS, NOW?

We planned a card game for later.
Favorite Syfy character Darth Vader.
Holding hands at the movie theater.
Enjoying each other eating popcorn.
Never leaving me stranded in life's storm.
Skinny dipping at the break of dawn.
Kissing my wet body and squeezing my arm.
Petals of young love being born.
Saying our vows before a priest, a lifetime that will grow and happiness forever form.
Pages of laughter and sunshine kept scared never ripped or torn.
A highway of love and raindrops of we can.
Pallbearers have lowered my casket in the ground, at my grave you stand.
Looking at family photos in the beginning, in the den pretending we are holding hands.
Conquering the world together was our plan.
Until she came along, and you broke our happy home and the sacred unity of our wedding band.
You are holding pieces of jewelry and my clothes; left behind I am covered by waves and lay beneath earth grains of dirt grains of sand.
You are searching for me in this place; when I was here my presence you ran.
Right side of the bed where I used to lay reaching for me now, then you were an unfaithful husband.

Visiting my grave talking for hours, when I was sick in the hospital you were busying holding her hand.

Hurting dying wanting a little of your time, too busy with her I did not understand.

Death doors has scattered pieces of me peacefully over the land.

Sniffing perfume on my clothes I would spray.

Reminiscing of little things, I would say.

Cards and letters interest, you now, moth eaten like bales of hay.

Appointments to be with you, my presence you avoided each day.

Seeds of life in my womb the hands of time blew away.

In the ground now and you decide to pray.

Sitting in my rocking chair is not going to bring me back.

Sweeping the leaves off the front porch; drinking sweet lemonade.

I am gone and there is nothing to bargain or trade.

Leaving me to be with her, past decisions already made.

Reaching for you ;I lay in our bed with covers pulled over your head.

Thinking of all the lies you said.

Our home beautiful, big, and lonesome it is open doors I dread.

Teary pillow blanket of truth our marriage is dead.

Kisses from you to me the winds blew to another.

In the hospital no family, mother, sister, or brother.

Lord please, pour clouds of comfort on my fragile body that is weak.

I prayed you come squeeze my arm or kiss my cheek.

Vows of love you no longer wanted to keep.

Behind the shower curtain; I cannot pull back smile and peek.

Letting go of her and holding onto me it is too late.

I am not on the back porch; I am not tying a bell on the front gate.

I am not in the back room getting ready for our movie date.

Not in the kitchen fixing your plate.

Switching channels or movies on cable.

Making dinner setting the table.

Simple things I used to do, because of this I am not able.

Its name I do not want to know; because dying alone I am, its name unknown on the label.

This life has no more hope; out of it painfully swiftly I will float.

Books I have read and written notes.

My pains will disappear being hung by death's rope.

I will be gone like dying cells; once seen through a microscope.

Bitterness is mines alone, holding onto us like the wind I foolishly hoped.

Her answers were kisses of yes; and mine your turned back and nope.

I know...

You will manage, because you have her and in time you will cope.

Resting in my grave, you are looking for me.

Forgetting my patience and endurance, my tears of hope for us you refused to see.

It does not matter how often you visit; in your world I can never be.

Truth you would not listened for raindrops of hope for us but, the voices of others and Ms. Shirley.

Goodbye my love, wings of life are broken, and you are finally free.

I forgive you because my husband you did not want to be.

My spirit hopes that you are happy.

When I was back there and alone, today it is too late for an apology.

Prayers of forgiveness from the heavens in your heart lies the key.

Memories of us are clouds of falling trees.

Us can never reunite, no more than burning leaves.

I can no longer listen to the beauty of the birds or humming bees.

I am dying alone and its excruciating pain.

Lord pop the vessels in my brain!

Where are you, death pointed fingers destiny I blame.

So unbearable each drop like hateful rain.

Tears of hope...you never came.

When I am gone at my grave you will try to explain.

I am not mad at you because you do not love me the same.

Shirley is the one to talk to, where I am, I cannot hear you call my name.

Live your life, I free you from infidelities, guilt and shame.

THE WIND...LISTEN MANKIND

We walked on a dirt road with trees saluting Him.
Roots giving Him praises and hallelujah shouts the oceans' waves.
The clouds sits underneath His feet.
His angels know where the four corners of the earth meet.
His breath pushes me upon the silent waters.
Into the His atmosphere I bow before Him.
From the heavens above I enjoy all the beauty He made below.
Into the ground seeds grow.
His heart is filled with tears for tomorrow.
Taken by the winds, that He could only create.
Making no mistakes, He is sorrowful for forming man.
I asked Him if He wanted me to blow them away?
If only man would seek My face…
I AM all he needs.
Everything that was made I made; it is beautiful.
Man is more than all the earth's beauty; because he is formed in My image.
Million waterfalls capturing the sun rising and going down cannot compare
To the breath I breathe in man.
The world cries because man is destroying it, including himself.
I will blow all the evil men away and viruses, threats and bombs will
blossom no more.
Matthew 5;18 'for verily I say unto you, Till heaven and earth pass, one
jot or tittle
Shall in no wise pass from the law, till all be fulfilled.'
Leave them be.

His voice was heavier than the earth's metal's. and softener than mountains of cotton.

Glancing at the world, it is evil and all that is attached tears from heaven began to form

A new ocean: an Ocean of Hurt for all the ones that were damned and did not care.

He pushed me toward the last days and the poisons released in the heavens and disease's

Being created by man…and his mountain of lies. Experimenting on billons thinking

He is more than Me

My Light will soon be taken from this world.

Oceans and multiple waves, I was there looking through, man's true mirror of Judgement.

I was blown to the beginning when the world was form and void.

Everything was black, to me beautiful. He created everything first and man was last because

He was given inner Light from God placing His beautiful soul within man.

Before all this He knew it would come to man's true mirror of Judgement soon.

Ezekiel 33;11 say unto them as I live says the Lord God, I have no pleasure in the death of the wicked,

I felt His presence with each stirring winds.

Thanking Him for making me and knowing He is Love.

He made everything out of His Love.

If only man would embrace.

Seeking God's wondrous face.

Because He has prepared a place for those who are His.

John 14;3 and if I go and prepare a place for you, I will come again and receive you unto myself. That where I am there ye may be also.

THEY SAID

The color of my eyes were too dark and deep.
The clothes I wear are raggedy and cheap.
Better if I died in my sleep.
These hateful words daily, others would speak
My appearance is the perfect picture of a freak.
Pushing me down, the inner me they kicked.
Hateful words daily...
My legs and arms was an infirmity.
I was not from either side of life's tracks.
Aliens dropped me off because of my looks, no intentions to retrieve me.
Friends I could count between my thumb and index finger.
I could not be a cheerleader; because being ugly is not anything to cheer about.
I tried out for track my legs would cramp up.
A sticky note on my blouse labeled black monkey.
Being kicked and made fun of every day.
Starring at the clock praying petals of beauty upon my face within these lonely hours.
If only my unpleasantness the clouds would wash away with its showers.
If my roots were in a rose garden, I would be beautiful because there are no ugly flowers.
Who I am is kind and caring, but my shell is what others see.
I have no purpose; my tears cannot save the roots of a dead tree.
There is no rays of smiles, only thorns behind a fallen façade.
The javelin I enjoyed until coach said I did not have what it takes.

I love to swim; my wings could not stretched because I was labeled black death.

Instruments amazed me until my music teacher told me they are to be handled by beautiful people.

School photographer, please do not waste your time smiling.

Went to church, I wanted to teach, the children would be afraid of me.

Loving words told to me by the pastor.

Not knowing God, I ran into a field of un-prejudiced flowers.

Hoping their beauty would rub on me.

Listening to the hummingbirds, if only their tune I could sing.

Peace from people, sunshine, here I can dream.

Capitellar turns into a beautiful butterfly.

Looking in the mirror I want to die.

Snails hiding within its shell.

Odd looking rocks I gather in my painful pail.

Alone unhappy not pretty dying in their hateful hell.

It is too much for me, I am tired, and all of my ugly self is a true story for them to someday tell.

Goodbye beauty, in your mirror I could never be.

Let me die here amongst this beauty.

Maybe something worthy will grow from me.

I am what…

They said….

TRAFFIC

Family of 6, 2 horses and a parakeet name Willie.
Whether my dad was on the highway or freeway work was
The direction he was mostly headed.
Both parents working over 84 hours a week not including dad's pop-up
Mandatory weekends.
One of his simplest pleasures are watching cars pass by.
Last week dad sitting on the balcony wiping tears from his eyes.
I was peeping through the blinds…
I know the smile on his face for us is covering hidden truths inside.
My brothers and I have everything we need and more.
Mom's on maternity leave, she is having a girl.
Mood swings and her unpredictable hormones hope we get through.
No nanny hired; we are taken care of.
Dad has come home, with a bag of sweets for mom,
And its wee hours of the night, soon being replaced with the morning sun.
In the kitchen, dad's sitting on the edge of the barstool; I give him a
big hug.
I know he is tired, working all the time and the loss of overdue relaxation and
Sleep.
Working hard, my dad would find water in a dry well.
Alone on the balcony, his peaceful cell.
Son, do not worry all is taken care of, from the mortgage to my boys
Jordan's Dolce& Gabbana
And Christian Louboutin yawl wear on your feet.

Work for dad is like the hands on the clock, quick shower, and bites of food he eats.

Looking in his eyes I feel his heart; He says son I get you.

What I do for you all is not something I was missing from my childhood because

I was poor.

I had loving parents and the song they sang daily in my heart work hard for what you

Want, if you do wrong things to get it; then you do not need it.

On life's concrete pavement, your smiles, hugs, and every occasion, including

Sitting by the pool, or on the porch, I see at every stop sign, red light,

Intersection and U-turn, prolonged board meetings, those moments mean the most.

Drinking a glass of milk and leaving his half-eaten toast.

If something should happen to me my five children will be taken care

Of after you all are grown.

I lived in a shack, condo, and a house on top of the hill, love is what makes it a home.

Dad, I am not worried about things, it is you are working all the time.

Remember son love can hold together all broken pieces, another song

From my parents, daddy smiling.

Watching dad leave the driveway.

I love you should have been words from me.

A thought… I should put a love you note, and I am proud you are my dad

On his dashboard.

Nah…. he is ok

Time has come dad decorated the house and went overboard.

With us boys' parties combined cannot compare to our sister's celebration.

I think that is what he needs an angel in the mist of all us roughed boys.

Today she will be here balloons and girly things of all colors have taken

Empty space filled with love.

Family and friends in the waiting room. Many having to go

Go to our house

Dad's in the delivery room, I know he is holding mom's hand.

When our sister gets here, I will tell dad I am proud of him and love him.

Dad was crying tears of joy, I did not get to tell him, he must have forgotten
Something in the car.
He will be back with a pink or yellow stuffed animal he brought yesterday
at Toys r us.
The pastor is speaking, and little Sarah is crying loud.
What should have been a beautiful christening is our dad's
Funeral, he got in and unexplainable accident being the only fatality.
Putting my hand in the pocket of my suit, a wrinkled note I got off his
dashboard
Saying I get you son and love you always.
I am back at the house peeping through the blinds, but I go sit besides
Him and hug him, but he disappears.
Sitting in his favorite spot on the balcony watching cars pass by
I wonder the many lanes in his hurting mind, and hoping love will hold
it together.
Sarah placed in his arms for a second, I guess love could not.
Tears of joy I saw was life's façade uncovered.
No matter how fast or slow we travel, we are all in traffic,
I hope none of you get traffic jammed like my loving dad.
When faced with bittersweet truth, love was not able to
Hold it together, because hurt was more.
I know he tried to give love a chance.
That day on the balcony was truth, no way possible, loving
Father and devoted husband miracles are not in his lane.
Loving us through it all and trying to carry truth's pain.
4 years ago, he got a vasectomy.
Flowers I place on his grave, his view of the freeway.
His peaceful time watching cars passing.
Now they are passing by him.
Time has come to the end of life's road; my dad was truly my angel.
All the memories of this hurt are no more.
Just for the ones left behind who utterly understands.
I love you always dad.

TRUTH

Do not need eye shadow or mascara.
Do not need to be covered.
Do not need extensions.
Do not need a face-lift.
Do not need your opinions'.
Do not need to be debated.
Do not need to be sugarcoated.
Do not need a crowd.
Do not have respect of person's.
Truth stands alone; and is not lonely.
Truth is Truth and not lukewarm.
Truth never changes.
Truth is the beginning of life.
Truth is the ending of darkness.
Truth is infinity.
Truth will not be silenced.
Truth after billions of years, equals Truth.
Truth is love.
Truth is not always smooth.
Truth knows you… Matthew 10:30, But even the hairs of
Your head are all numbered.
Truth hurts sometimes, if applied daily the end is glorious
Truth can be trusted through everything.
Truth will keep you and never forsake you.
Truth, John 14:2, In my Father's house are many mansions; if

It were not so; I would have told you. I go to prepare a place for you.
John14:3, And if I go and prepare a place for you, I will come again, and
Receive you unto Myself; that where I am, ye maybe also.
Truth's road is narrow and straight always.
Truth is innocent, even though man said Truth was guilty.
Truth sacrificed its life for a world of guilty people.
Truth is genuine love even in the face of a horrible suffering death.
Luke 23:34…
"Forgive them Father, for they know not what they do".
Truth has a place prepared for believers of the Truth.
Truth invited you to attend, the wedding of the Lamb.
Truth is Alpha and Omega
Truth's judgement's are fair.
Truth, love, longsuffering, patience, faith.
Truth path leads to everlasting life for all.
Revelation 3:10, Because you have kept My word about patient,
Endurance, I will keep you from the hour of trial that is coming
On the whole world, to try those who dwell on the earth.
James 1:12, Blessed is the man who remains steadfast under trial,
For when he has stood the test, he will receive the crown of life,
Which YAH has promised those who love Him.
Truth knew you from the beginning.
Truth, Jeremiah 1:5, Before I formed you in the womb, I knew you.
Job 23:10, But He knows the way I take, when He has tried me,
I shall come out as gold.
Truth… John 3:16, For YAH so loved the world, that He gave
His only begotten Son, that whosoever believeth in Him should
Not perish but have everlasting life.
Truth is John 4:24, YAH is spirit, and those who worship Him
Must worship Him in Spirit and Truth.

WANT TO MEET YOU, LORD

Lord I want to meet You.
Lord I want to meet You.
I want meet the One who gave Moses the strength to part the Red Sea.
I want to meet the one who talked through the burning bush.
I need to meet You Lord.
I do not need to meet Oprah Winfrey.
I do not need to meet Tyler perry
Lord I need to meet you
I do not need to meet the president
I want to meet the One who set my soul free.
I do not need to meet any famous celebrity.
I do not need to meet the queen of England.
I need to meet You.
I need to meet the One who cleansed my sinful slate.
I do not need to meet the rich souls of the world, Jeff Bezos, Bill Gates, or
the Rockefeller family.
I want to meet the One who died on Calvary.
I want to meet You.
I do not need to meet the Pope or anyone who teaches purgatory.
I want to meet the One who hung and died for me.
Lord I want to meet You
Lord I want to meet You.

YESTERDAY'S WORLD...
TODAY'S PEOPLE

Stories my great great-grandfather told.

Lord keep their suffering restless souls.

The corn is yellow and the rows of cotton hundred miles of white.

The land stretched further than the light.

Man plowing in the field before dawn and past the night.

Bondage, slavery it is their laws, used like a machine everything's wrong and nothing is right.

Man put man in chains, because of his darkened skin.

Iron around our necks, chained hands, and feet, headed toward our end.

Freedom we cried. I am a slave because of my ancestors' sins.

Cramped in the bottom of ships destined to being disrespected, tortured, and our manhood taken.

The only question never asked, how long Lord will we be forsaken?

They raped our men and women, hoping through our children's eyes this truth the heaven will have shaken.

Blistered hands, limbs cut off, lives taken.

Blooded bodies and weaken broken backs.

Days I hate I wad given this cursed skin of black.

Justice, Love, and Equality pushes us off its tracks.

Out of the womb no light, being engulfed in fear!

Four corners of the earth, bondage trapped within disobedience sphere.

Running, traveling in this wilderness asking God why must we remain here?

Our women belong to them, our children eyes open wide.

Freedom, hope, laughter, peace, our ancestors lied!

Prisoners', slaves in their world, years from now will still be sadness, nothing to joke about being funny.

Where is the land flowing with milk and honey?

Their world hate, greed, and the love of money.

Great-great-grandfather being beat and tortured because he refused to cry.

Horror, true stories told to me I cry.

Where is God?

He's holding me; close pray my Child, there is beauty beyond the heavens and above the sky.

We are a blessed people, whether we are generation hundredth sixth, seventh or eighth, God don't put too much on our plates.

We shall overcome, we have the strength our faith!

Black, yellow, red, brown blessed from birth.

It is not about darkened skin but, disobedience that scattered us to the four corners of the earth.

YOU

You chose me out of billions.
You laughed in my errors of life.
You rejoiced in my clouds of sorrows.
You danced in my defeats.
You took my blanket of protection.
Underneath the world saw my nakedness.
Daily I drank from the cup of shamefulness.
You pushed me onto a freeway; during its busiest hours.
You cut my petals, leaving little root for growth.
You stood in front of the sun,
After its rays burned my flesh.
You took my training wheels off too soon.
You put me on a path blindfolded,
We climbed the mountain; and by Your hands pushed me over.
My dreams and accomplishments You buried at the bottom of life's
waterfall.
Food from heaven and its abundance, I ate fallen crumbs.
My clouds of light smothered within its Death of Spring.
The rooster crows at the midnight hour of dawn,
In its cemented cemetery my body lay.
You whipped my bruised body out of anger and hate.
You put me in a field with its cursed rows of scorched earth.
I hate the day; from my mother's womb I was birthed!
You placed a wondrous oasis before my eyes; within a blink a disappearing
mirage.

You gave my seas and oceans of hope; attached prolonged years drowning, within its depths of pain and betrayal.

You gave me my bride,

And another was the one she desired.

My seeds you cursed, her lover his flourished like the stars in the sky.

Days, weeks, months, years, I cried.

Wishing you would have closed my mother's womb.

What have I done to deserve all this darkness?

Who am I?

Why did You do this to me?

YHWH answers...

Why YESHUA, Why Calvary?

Why not you?

My tool chosen out billions and billions of souls?

Because I love you.

Tried in the firer.

You shall come forth like refined gold.

In My arms; that glorious day, you I will eternally hold.

My child…

Everlasting joy and beauty for you is my eternal desire!

Printed in the United States
by Baker & Taylor Publisher Services